What Is the Media?

by Julia Jones

HOUGHTON MIFFLIN   BOSTON

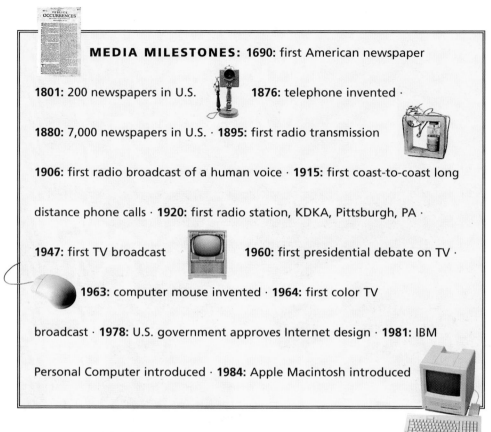

MEDIA MILESTONES: **1690:** first American newspaper

1801: 200 newspapers in U.S. **1876:** telephone invented ·

1880: 7,000 newspapers in U.S. · **1895:** first radio transmission

1906: first radio broadcast of a human voice · **1915:** first coast-to-coast long

distance phone calls · **1920:** first radio station, KDKA, Pittsburgh, PA ·

1947: first TV broadcast **1960:** first presidential debate on TV ·

1963: computer mouse invented · **1964:** first color TV

broadcast · **1978:** U.S. government approves Internet design · **1981:** IBM

Personal Computer introduced · **1984:** Apple Macintosh introduced

The Media Around Us

We use the word *media* to mean two different things. It can mean ways of communicating information — from newspapers to computers. It can also mean the people whose job is to bring us information, especially reporters and broadcasters.

We are surrounded by many different media, but they add up to *one* powerful force in our lives. By knowing how the media works, we can make good use of it and keep from being controlled by it.

Print Media

Newspapers

Newspapers have been voices of news and opinion since the 1600s. They showed their importance in the American colonies in 1735. Peter Zenger criticized the governor of New York in his newspaper. He was arrested, but a jury found him innocent. Americans showed that they valued freedom of the press.

In the 1800s the "penny newspaper" became even more popular. Then, after the telegraph came along, newspapers began reporting the news more quickly and reliably. By 1880, there were 7,000 newspapers in the United States.

As the twentieth century began, newspapers were the source for information. But could that information be trusted? Early newspapers often reflected the opinions of their publishers, even in the way they told the news. However, after the Civil War the facts became more important. News stories stressed the "five w's" — *who, what, when, where,* and *why*. Opinions were still important, but they tended to stay on the editorial pages.

Newspapers grew rapidly in the 1900s. They now included photographs, sports sections, and color comics. They were also big business. The publishers Joseph Pulitzer and William Randolph Hearst tried different ways to attract more readers. Pulitzer sent a reporter, Nellie Bly, around the world. Her journey became a big story.

Soon a few publishers began buying up newspapers across the country. E.W. Scripps created the first large chain of newspapers. By 1929, the Scripps-Howard chain owned twenty-five newspapers. The few newspaper chains became very powerful. They could take sides on an issue. One writer said, "Freedom of the press is for those who own one."

Many newspapers have tried to build a reputation for reporting that is unbiased — that tells the news without taking sides. *The Washington Post*, *The New York Times*, and *The Los Angeles Times* are three examples.

However, fewer people get their news through the newspaper today. In 1946, 85% of Americans read a newspaper every day. In a 1999 survey, only 21% of Americans could say that.

Magazines

The first English magazines, in the 1700s, looked like books. Instead of the news of the day, they contained stories and articles and did not include advertising. Early magazines like *The Spectator* were so expensive that only rich people could afford to buy them. Because of the way magazines were printed, only about 100,000 copies could be published. Then a new printing press was invented that could print millions of copies in full color. This made magazines ideal for advertising and reaching a big audience.

Advertising gave magazines a big boost in the 1900s. By 1930, magazines were riding high on the money companies paid to advertise their products. The magazines were able to lower their prices, so many more people could buy them. Magazines gave advertisers a good way to sell products. Magazines became slick and colorful.

Automobile advertisement, c. 1913

Different magazines were made to suit many different interests. There were magazines like *Life* that covered the news of the week, using photographs by the best photographers of the day. There were magazines that specialized in fashion, sports, literature, business, politics, farming, and movie stars.

The companies who advertised in magazines sometimes affected what went in them. Magazines might not include articles that an advertiser did not like. They were afraid they would lose the advertising dollars. For example, tobacco companies advertised widely in magazines. The first magazine article about the dangers of cigarettes did not appear until 1979 in a brave magazine called *Mother Jones*.

Today there are magazines for runners, dog lovers, cat lovers, knitters, bicyclists, artists, history buffs — you name it. This is a perfect situation for advertisers. They can find, or target, the exact people they think will want to buy certain products.

Telecommunications

Telephones

In the 1870s, the telephone allowed people to be their own broadcasters, not in Morse Code but "person to person."

The first telephone system had a lot of problems. Few people had phones in their homes. Most people had to wait in line to use one at a store or other public place. There was no long distance service. The sound was poor and the service was not reliable.

By 1906 people were able to talk over a distance of 1,000 miles. By 1915 the East and West Coasts were connected by telephone.

Once telephone service was in place, telephone companies focused on improving it. Insulated wire and automatic switching stations made phone service better. Lines were extended to reach more people.

Wooden telephone, c. 1907

In 1950, 75% of all telephone lines were "party lines." People shared the same line. One person could not use the phone if someone else on that line was already using it.

In 1960, the American Telephone and Telegraph Company set up the first electronic switching station. This allowed more calls to go through, faster. People now had private lines.

After 1975, telephone technology advanced at a dizzying rate. Long distance service had been so costly that people only used it for special occasions or emergencies. It went down to a few cents a minute. Fax machines became common in the early 1980s. They allowed written text to be sent over telephone lines.

Today telephone lines hook up to the Internet and send e-mail. The telephone is a medium that has changed with the times.

Cell Phones

In 1947, researchers began experimenting with the idea of sending phone messages without wires to different locations or "cells." Finally, on April 3, 1973, Martin Cooper of the Motorola Company placed the first cell phone call. A new age of portable phones was born.

The first cell phone was big and bulky. It weighed almost two pounds. Plus, the government had strict radio and telephone regulations about who could use radio airwaves. These rules were put in place before cell phones. It took time to change the rules.

Using a cell phone

Eventually, low-cost microprocessors, or small computer chips, made cell phones smaller. Improvements in using radio frequencies made phones more reliable.

Today there are over sixty million cell phone users. The industry earns over $30 billion a year. Now you can send e-mails and text messages on your cell phone. You can take a photograph and send it to someone. You can play games on your phone through the Internet. And you can call anyone from almost anywhere.

Radio

Radio was first used for navigation. It allowed ships to contact other ships or people on land. When the *Titanic* sank in 1912, radio helped other ships find survivors. World War I delayed radio as a means of mass communication. The government wanted to keep the airwaves clear.

But by the mid-1920s radio stations were being built across America. The Radio Corporation of America, or RCA, began making radios that most people could afford. Soon there was a radio in everyone's living room.

Early radio programs were mostly news and music. Before long, programs included comedy, variety, dramas, mysteries, baseball, and quiz shows. Families would gather around the radio in the evening and listen together. Advertisers could count on a wide audience to hear their commercials.

Radio had its Golden Age from 1933 to 1950. During the years of the Depression, President Franklin Roosevelt broadcast "fireside chats" over the radio to comfort Americans. During World War II, Americans were able to keep up with the latest events in Europe and the Pacific.

After the war, the radio business boomed. The number of radio stations more than doubled in just three years. Six million cars were built with radios. Radio was the main source of news for 63% of Americans.

A family listening to the radio, 1930

By 1950, forty million American homes had at least one radio. Half of the 2,000 radio stations were part of three major networks — the American Broadcasting Company (ABC), the National Broadcasting Company (NBC), and the Columbia Broadcasting System (CBS).

Then came television.

Television

Commercial television broadcasting began in the United States in 1947. Television programs were broadcast in black and white. Many of the early programs were taken from network radio. Radio stars like Jack Benny and Lucille Ball became just as popular on TV.

Between 1953 and 1955, Americans fell in love with television. Programs began to change. *Today*, a magazine-like show on NBC, started in 1952. ABC made its first profits from shows for children such as *The Mickey Mouse Club*. As with radio, advertisers, or sponsors, were able to target their audience, for example, advertising toys for Saturday morning children's programs.

Television also changed politics. What people saw often made a different impression from what they heard. The first presidential debate on television was between John F. Kennedy and Richard M. Nixon in 1960. Kennedy appeared handsome and calm. Nixon looked nervous and unattractive. People who

Walter Cronkite delivers the news from his CBS Television studio.

listened to the debate on the radio said that Nixon had won. People who watched on TV preferred Kennedy. Politicians learned to use television to their advantage.

In 1964, color broadcasting began on prime-time television. TV became even more appealing. News programs grew in importance.

The War in Vietnam was the first war to unfold on television. People saw footage of battles and what the war was like for the soldiers. The government tried to tell people one version of how the war was going. But people could see another. Television helped to change public opinion of the war.

Today television brings the world into our homes. Instead of getting events filtered through a newspaper or magazine article, we can see what happens when it happens. In turn, this can affect how we think and feel about what's going on in the world.

According to studies by the U.S. Department of Education, the typical American watches television for four hours a day. At that rate, by the time a person is sixty-five, he or she will have spent a total of nine years watching television.

Computer Technology

Computers

The early computers of the 1950s and 1960s were so large they took up an entire room. They were hard to program, could solve only one problem at a time, and couldn't store large amounts of information. Computers were useful to NASA for the space program. But could they ever be very useful to other people?

Early computer called the Pilot ACE, Britain, 1950

Thanks to computer pioneers like Grace Hopper, the answer was *yes*. Hopper, an officer in the U.S. Navy, developed a process that led to user-friendly computer languages. This opened the door for more computer uses and users.

In 1963 the computer mouse was patented. It allowed users to "point and click" and made operating a computer much easier.

Intel introduced a computer microchip in 1971. It led to a new generation of high technology, or computer-based, products.

IBM came out with its first PC (personal computer) in 1981. Apple Computer introduced the Macintosh in 1984. It was the first truly user-friendly personal computer.

In 1990, Microsoft introduced an operating system called Windows. It made using a PC easy. Now, anyone could use a PC for writing, creating, and figuring things out. And millions do.

The Internet

The idea of the World Wide Web, or Internet, began in the 1950s. The Internet started out as a tool for research centers. It allowed computers to share information over wires. The possibilities for the public were enormous. What if everyone's computer could be linked to sources of information and entertainment!

Many different people helped make that vision real by writing new computer programs and developing new equipment. The U.S. government accepted the final design in 1978.

In 1981, a group of graduate students at the University of Illinois invented a "browser" program called Mosaic, which made searching the Internet easier.

Tim Berners-Lee invented HTML (hyper-text markup language) in 1989. This new language made it easy to get information from the Internet.

The Internet has changed education, business, and personal communications. It allows people to share information with others halfway around the world.

Messaging, Blogs, and E-zines

Computer technology has given us a wide variety of media just for the computer.

Instant messaging, or IM, uses the Internet to allow people to send messages immediately. The system tells you when someone on your "buddy list," or the people that you choose to IM with, are online and trying to contact you. You can then start a "chat" session where you type messages back and forth.

Blogs, short for "web logs," are a blend of personal diary and web guide. Blogs are locations on the Internet where an individual or a group of "bloggers" can keep a journal of thoughts, opinions, or activities. Blogs offer people a chance to express ideas together. Sometimes those ideas can be a powerful force for change. News reporters and politicians pay attention to what bloggers are thinking.

A girl using a webcam (video camera) sends her friend an instant message.

E-zines are Internet or e-mail newsletters or magazines. They often help the visitors find other sources through links to other websites. Some e-zines come in both paper and electronic versions. You can subscribe to an e-zine and have it delivered to your e-mail box. Some are free. Others you have to pay for.

The Future of Media

We think of the media as many different kinds of communication, with each one staking out its own territory. But the future of media depends on their joining forces. We already see it happening in the following examples.

- Many newspapers have websites where the newspapers can be viewed on the Internet. Some newspapers are also looking at sending their site directly to e-mail addresses. Magazines are also making Internet versions. Formatting is as important on the screen as it is on paper. The Internet version must be fun to look at and easy to get through.
- Telephones will continue to change with the times. All telephones will be wireless. They will be small personal computers. They will have large calendars, address books, and computer programs.
- Television technology will improve. The Federal Communications Commission (FCC) has required that starting in 2004 all new TVs must have HDTV, or high-definition, technology.
- Radio is going digital. The new technology is known as High Definition (HD) Radio. The fancier name is In-Band On-Channel Digital Audio Broadcasting. It makes the sound much better. Stations come in more clearly. You can listen to digital stations nationwide.
- Computer technology will continue to get better and cheaper. More and more people will be able to afford a computer. The technology will combine with cell phones to be mobile.

In many ways, the media is how we will imagine the future.